The Later Verses of Frank Arcanity

Scenes from a fictional life

Also by Michael H. Dickman:

Acrostica volumes I–IV

The Later Verses of Frank Arcanity
Scenes from a fictional life

by **Michael H. Dickman**

with illustrations by

Karina Arreola and **Jarett Coyle**

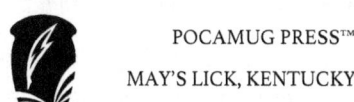

POCAMUG PRESS™
MAY'S LICK, KENTUCKY

Published by Pocamug Press™
5037 Alhambra Rd.
Mayslick, KY 41055
www.pocamug.com
Version date 5/22/16

Text copyright © 2016 by Michael H. Dickman
Photographs on page 9 © 2016 by Michael H. Dickman
Illustrations on pages 12, 37, 54, and 80 © 2016 by Karina Arreola
Illustrations on pages 19, 57, 61, 69, and 93 © 2016 by Jarett Coyle
All rights reserved.
This is a work of fiction. Some events depicted are based on actual occurrences but are not a factual account. Any resemblance of the fictional characters to real people is coincidental.

Library of Congress Control Number: 2016937878

ISBN-13: 978-0-9908877-7-5
ISBN-10: 0-990887774

Cover photos by Amanda Hankinson

Cover design by Karina Arreola

The lightning-quill-in-a-jar colophon
is a trademark of Pocamug Press.

There is really no fiction or nonfiction; there is only narrative.

– E. L. Doctorow

The Pocamug Press Emerging Artist Series spotlights writers, illustrators, and other artists who are being published for the first time in a particular genre. This is the initial book in the series, featuring the first published book of poetry by Michael H. Dickman and the first book illustrations by Karina Arreola and Jarrett Coyle.

Contents

List of Illustrations	1
Foreword	3
Introduction	5
Forgotten Symmetry	7
Child in Bathtub	13
Books, Books, Books	17
Adult Education	20
Becoming Rehinged	22
The Forgiving	34
Love Sum	38
Stay Alive	42
Conventional Poem	44
Throwing Pots	48
We Only Talked	50
You Fall In Love	55
The Alchemy of Pain	59
Lost Child	63
My Mother	64
My Father	70
We Will Meet Again	76
The Uniform	81

Notes	87
Epilogue	95
About the Author	99
About the Illustrators	101
You're a Fire	102
Acknowledgments	103
Reading Group Guide	104
Afterword	107

List of Illustrations and Photos

Illustrations by Karina Arreola:

Child in Bathtub	12
The Forgiving	37
You Fall in Love	54
The Uniform	80

Illustrations by Jarett Coyle:

Books, Books, Books	12
You Fall in Love	57, 93
The Alchemy of Pain	61
My Mother	69

Photos on page 9:

(Top) Road marker near the birthplace of Albert Sidney Johnston in Old Washington, Kentucky

(Bottom) Headstone at the grave of William "Bull" Nelson in Maysville, Kentucky

Foreword

I am pleased to present the later verses of Frank Arcanity. The various details of the circuitous route this work traveled, starting from loose pages found after Frank's untimely death to finished manuscript, are not worth mentioning. Fortunately I was able to find someone who knew Frank during the time some of these pieces were written, and convinced him to write whatever notes he could to help put some context into the bare lines.

The subjects range over the lifetime of an unknown writer. The notes will no doubt shed light where no other source of illumination is possible. Mr. Dechante was the only person available who could explicate some of Frank's more obscure passages. The editor will add the notes at the end of the book.

Poetry-as-fiction is not so unusual. Less often does it claim to be a fictional autobiography. An even smaller subset would contain semi-autobiographical material recast as fiction written by a pseudonymous janitor. One could attempt to go further down this particular rabbit-hole but fortunately I am running out of space on the page. Arguably, all autobiography is reality-based fiction. As the old saying doesn't go, there are lies, damned lies, statistics, and autobiography. Is any of this true? Perhaps that's the wrong question.

Michael H. Dickman   April, 2016

Introduction

William Johnson who took the name Frank Arcanity was born on May 12, 1952 in Cincinnati, Ohio, and died of acute alcohol poisoning November 10, 2013 in Las Vegas, Nevada. He had worked a series of odd jobs most of his life.

Frank lived with his parents until he was thirty, moving when he was eighteen into their basement which had previously been a rec room. He attended college while living at home. He never graduated.

Little is known of his life between the ages of thirty and fifty-five, as he was estranged from his family. In 2007 he started working in a Las Vegas casino as a janitor. I first met him in 2010 at a tiki bar on Charleston Boulevard, where he was writing some of the works presented here. I got to know him as well as anyone did. Later, when I was asked to provide insight and background for this book I was not enthusiastic. However, I realized there were some things I could say here that might otherwise be ignored, so I accepted the task.

Many of the pieces seem straightforward enough but the obvious interpretations run counter to what we know about him. I will attempt to note, in commentary for some of the pieces, those details of Frank's life, as told to me, that may have prompted the creation of his brief and cryptic oeuvre.

Samuel Dechante   April 2016

Forgotten Symmetry

(Prologue)

Forgotten, all forgotten.

— Why?

Because of Sputnik, the Great Depression, Kennedy's Assassination, the Great War, 9/11, Hippies. Nobody remembers a man born in Kentucky, moved to Texas, fought against Santa Anna, and then in the Utah War.

— The Utah War?

Forgotten. He moved to California, joined the Confederacy when Texas did, commanded troops at Shiloh.

— I remember Shiloh.

Liar. He was shot in the back of the knee, didn't realize he was bleeding out. Shot accidentally by one of his own men, likely. Bleeding into his boot. See, there on his horse, as he surveys the battle, thinking he'll find a surgeon later, his boot in its stirrup filling with his thick, red life.

— Who was he?

Albert Sidney Johnston. Might have been the best commander the South had. Nobody said, Well there goes our Peculiar Institution, as the liquid started to spill, as it spread over the warming April ground and he fell down dead.

— Is there more?

Of course. In strange symmetry, William "Bull" Nelson born a few miles away from Johnston. Also fought in Mexico, fought at Shiloh too but for the Union.

— Shot in the knee?

Don't be ridiculous. Shot at Louisville's Galt House later that year by Jefferson Davis.

— The Confederate President?

No, shot by Jefferson C. Davis, a Union officer who was at Fort Sumter with Abner Doubleday during the war's very beginning.

— The inventor of baseball?

Rather, the inventor of the San Francisco cable car. Doubleday never invented baseball. Both men, Johnston and Nelson, two of the best, both killed by people on their own side. Both now forgotten.

— Liar.

The Poems

Child in Bathtub

Child

Child in bathtub

Child in bathtub playing

Child in bathtub playing while mother washes him.

When you are a child everything is new

E v e r y t h i n g

The water is new

You hadn't noticed it before

How different it is from the tub

Different from you.

The whole world is different now.

Laughing, splashing

Hit the water with your hand

See how it sparkles

Makes your hand feel funny

Stop the mother says

You aren't sure what she means

You don't realize this but

Your splashes are getting her wet

Everything is new

And the world suddenly comes together

Laughing, splashing

And now you see that

Everything is

J o y o u s

Share the joy with your mother

Hit the water with your hand

If you were older you might say

This was when I first had a sense of self

Stop the mother says louder

If you were older you might say

This was when I first realized the world is joyous

Laughing, splashing

Hit the water with your hand

She lifts you out of the tub

She takes you by the shoulders and shakes you

She shakes you

She shakes you

Stop the mother screams

You stop laughing.

The whole world is different now

Something happened to you

The world is no longer joyous

You feel sick

You have to lie down

You start having bad dreams.

Later, they wonder why

You bang your head against the wall

Later, they wonder why

You scream with all your strength at odd times

As though you were splitting open to let something out

You don't know why, either.

Everything

Is new.

Books, Books, Books

The house is full of mysterious things
With pictures of cowboys and horses with wings
Books, books, books.

Your sister, she shows you that words can be read
You borrow a flashlight to read them in bed
Books, books, books.

Kindergarten teachers are caught off guard
By this child who reads them no matter how hard
Books, books, books.

The teachers say first grade would just be a waste
But the parents decide not to advance in such haste
Books, books, books.

They didn't ask him what he would prefer
Because a child to his parents must always defer
Books, books, books.

Well, first grade was a waste and second was too
Two years is one-third of your life for you
If you want to make your children bored with school
This is the only thing you have to do

Make certain they're held back every step of the way
So frustration and boredom will hold them in sway
And if ever it happens they're challenged one day
By math or history, or chemistry, say
Books, books, books
They won't know how to respond.

But it doesn't matter because school is boring
And they've found other things they can do
Like daydream and doodle
Make mischief and soon it'll
Be time to go home once again.

Yet if you are lucky
And have strength enough
To learn some things on your own
You'll find the pleasures, the riches, the treasures,
The infinite reaches from deserts to beaches
To skyscrapers, oceans, the planets and more,
Crusades, revolutions, economics, pollution,
And politics, science galore
In your own little universe there under the covers
Between and within, where else would you look?
In books, books, books.

Adult Education

(We Draw the Lines)

I told them, all men, all women,

Are cousins

Near and distant

I told them, race is an illusion

Rooted in undependable

And superficial perceptions.

They looked at me in disbelief

You are wrong, they said

It is obvious there are races, they said

Indignation in their raised voices

It's true there are differences, I said

(Trying to soothe feelings)

But they are minor, meaningless

They are important, they said

Our hair is different from theirs

Our skin is different from theirs

Our lips are different from theirs

You may think that, I said
But there are no lines you can draw
That will reliably corral these groups
To set them apart one from another

They looked at me with pity and disgust
We draw the lines, they said
And you had better pay attention to them.

Becoming Rehinged

Chemistry my joy, my joy was chemistry.
Fireworks, explosives, pyrotechnics,
Intoxicants, anesthetics, opiates, hallucinogens,
Flavors and fragrances, poisons and antidotes,

Fascinating subjects all.
How can everyone not be fascinated?
How can everyone not spend their time
Reading about chemistry
Reading about in-/organic chemistry
Reading about ethno-, psychopharmacology

And then I remember
That most people don't
Because most people can't
Because learning is something
They did when in school
And it takes time to earn a living.
Not everyone's interested
In learning about things

Even if those things

Determine their lives

In ways they don't even know.

It was the '60s, and

Experimenting with drugs

Was what many people did

But most of them

Didn't know

The smallest of facts

About the thing they were doing.

The irony was

Even if you had read

Everything you could

About LSD, mescaline,

Marijuana,

Mushrooms and morning glory,

Ayahuasca,

DMT, STP, and all the rest,

You still knew very little

Because the knowledge was forbidden

Because the research was forbidden

Because...?

Help me out here.

Because we don't want to know?

No, worse: because we are afraid

That if we knew the facts

We would see that many of our policies

About drugs

Are wrong, unfair, criminal.

At least, that's the way it often seems.

Some drugs really are bad. Speed kills.

Sniffing glue can cause brain damage.

Opiates make you stupid.

It requires a lot of reading

To be able to tell the difference

Between drugs that can kill you

And those that probably won't.

So does it surprise you

To know when I tell you

That I read everything I could

About marijuana,

Lysergic acid diethylamide,

Hashish, psylocibin, peyote; that
Mankind's been using them
For thousands of years
(Well, not LSD but that's
Just because it's new,
The others are ancient)
And then, knowing
That these drugs are not very dangerous...

(But wait, people who used these drugs
Stared into the sun or a toaster
Went blind or roasted their eyes like eggs
Went berserk and stabbed people
Thinking they were being attacked or worse,
Or threw themselves out windows, off roofs
Thinking they could fly.

My father once gave me a book about that
Maybe he saw my books on pharmacology
Suspected I wanted to experiment
Like so many others were doing
He had this book
With a friendly, trippy, paisley cover

And in it were horror stories

About what people did

When they took LSD

And suddenly went out of their minds.

It had no copyright information

That I recall

No author

No publisher

It was clearly a book meant to frighten

Not inform. All propaganda, all lies.

I gave him that book back

But I wish I had kept it

Just to put in a collection

Of anti-drug mania

Caused by fear of the unknown.

And let's not forget

The inevitable disclaimer

Don't take these drugs

When they are illegal

You might get arrested.

That could ruin your life

More likely than taking them would

They are not "safe"

Nothing is "safe"

You can drown in two inches of water.

You don't know what's in those

Black market drugs

It might be what's supposed to be in them

But maybe it isn't.

And it's too late to know

When you've fallen into a coma.

You might be allergic

To something that's in them

Other people taking them safely

But when it's your turn you swell up, turn red, vomit

You die horribly because

You didn't take my advice

To just say no.

And maybe you're just a little bit

Crazy already

Taking some of these drugs

Could push you over the edge

Never to return.

There, that should do it,

You're okay now, too frightened

To take drugs you buy on the street

And I can resume then to tell you my story

But remember, stay away from opiates if you can—

They really do make you stupid.)

...that my first trip was with three other people

They gave me only half a dose

Because I was a neophyte.

I studied the effects on myself

In my own way

Not very scientific

Later, I took it more often than was prudent

But stopped when I realized

My short-term memory

Was beginning to wander away.

I alarmed my parents once

They had two people over

I went to my room alone

Had planned to stay there

And observe the effects
Of LSD on myself
When I was alone

But then the couple upstairs
Started an argument between themselves
Somehow that struck me as funny
I went up there
To see what was happening
Suddenly no longer alone

The couple hurried out
I stayed a while with my parents
They knew that something was wrong

I shouldn't have told them
That I was tripping
But they didn't panic
Or raise an alarm
They did voice concern
But I love them for letting me
Deal with it, myself
Without involving hospitals or law.

I suppose it helped that I was

Fairly coherent

And did not panic, myself.

That night as I lay there

In bed not sleeping

I determined that some kind of good

Would result from my hasty actions.

I examined my thinking,

Decided to build from the ground up.

Threw out all the assumptions I could.

Left with the bare minimum of fact,

And asked myself the question

How do we know what is true?

That was my touchstone, my lighthouse, my bearing

That was the basis of building my structure,

My edifice of thought, my method of knowledge.

I spent all night building, going back

To the foundations, and building again to be sure

Going over each brick, every beam, every wall

To know logic would support the whole.

Hallucinogens can be social drugs
For humans are animals social
But let me suggest that the things that you think
When tripping, can inform your mind's patterns.

Now, maybe I've got it backwards, and
No amount of effort will reward you with result
But I tend to believe
That the effort succeeds
If your mind is prepared to a fault.

These drugs are not usually considered an aid
To logic or reason or thought
But then there's so much that we do not know
Would it surprise you that a drug that's
Supposed to leave you unhinged
Could be used to hinge yourself better?

But it's not easy
It's not a royal road
It's hard work
And there's no guarantee of success.

I stopped taking them decades ago

I no longer need to, or want to

Other things are more interesting now,

Creating and reading,

Playing and feeding

My imagination with books, music and film.

It's a marvelous place we live on, this earth

With spectacles, vastness, and beauty

But here I must leave you

The storyteller gets weary

The sun is going down and

Now the mosquitoes will eat me alive.

The Forgiving

Living away from home
For the first time in my life
Being responsible, doing
Laundry and cooking
Getting a sense of my life.

If you can manage it
Distance gives perspective,
Some way to consider anew
The things that have happened
The good and the bad
Everything that happened to you.

It isn't uncommon
To hate your parents
And love them both at once
Emotions are animals
Feed one, feed the other
And hope they don't tie us in knots.
It isn't uncommon
To blame your parents
For things you think they did wrong
But at some point

You must do things yourself
And take control of your life.

Your life becomes
Your responsibility
Regardless of what
Your mother and father did
And if you can do that,
Grow up and accept that
Then this is what you must do.

Forgive your parents
For whatever they did
Whether real or imagined and not,
If they loved you then love them
If they hated you then love yourself
And forgive them whichever way.

You cannot truly love another
Until you love yourself
So it was told to me one day
So I tell it here
It may be true.

I know enough to say—
Loving yourself

Is one important thing
You can do to change the world.

Not to say always be selfish
Not to say always be vain
But love and accept what you are
Be your own good parent
So you can be you
Not someone else's idea
Of what you should be

Then forgive your mother and father
Whatever they did or did not.
Forgive them.
Forgive them.
Forgive them.

Love Sum

These are the women I have loved.
Diane, whose father threw me out of the bedroom
(Before I even kissed her)
Cathy, who saw my first attempt at fiction
In seventh grade on the bus
Mary, with the butterfly tattoo (fake?)
On her dreamy thigh
I was too young, too shy to tell them.
My advice to my younger self: tell them
If you can.
They will know the love of a twelve-year-old boy
Is a sweet, precious, shallow thing
That will not likely survive the summer
But when the boy also knows that,
The telling becomes more difficult.
My advice to my younger self: tell them
Anyway.
Even if it is merely infatuation
Because being told you are loved
In the muck that is one's life
Is still sweet and precious
Even if it dies the next day.
Even if it is a lie.

Because love is always a lie
Especially when it is real.

Then there was A
Her sweet love lifted me
And B, whose hot love
Dragged me down
C who saved me but would not stay
D, who was there, and not there, and
There
And not there
E who was almost the one
F who had me and had me
Even though I didn't really want her to
G who played games
H — Oh, H. Sweetest of all,
And completely ruthless.
A force of nature
Her tenderness was her cruelty
A woman to pledge one's life to
Just before she brings the blade down.
My love for her was completely selfless
And completely doomed.

There is a pattern here, somewhere.
Too often they're already married or

They quickly get engaged
To somebody else.
J (because there is no "I" in Love),
We both knew it couldn't last
But it was fun to watch us burn
Too close to the fire.
K, we both thought it would last
But the fire went out
Whether from lack of fuel
Or smothered by age
It doesn't really matter now.
L, if you are reading this
You will know I died that night
But my love lives on. Zombie-like
It rises from the grave again
And again to haunt me
It's strange to be haunted by your own ghost
But even the ghost of my love for you
Is more real than I am now.

Love Sum (A..L) > Sum (A..L)
Subtract the pain
Divide by experience
Embrace the remainder.

Stay Alive

Your life is a story

Told by nobody

Without a plot

Dialogue written by others

Stay tuned for this important message

Your life is a commercial

Seen by nobody

Without a product

On sale nowhere

Back to our regularly scheduled program

Your life is a news item

Reported by nobody

Without a headline

Random actions ensue

Voiceover by thunder wind rain

No details at eleven

Your life is a docudrama

A new season starts

You've never seen this program before

It's just like all the others

But you'll enjoy it more

Your life is a sitcom

Without jokes

No actions ensue

The writers gave up

Because nothing is funny

Except maybe death.

He killed himself one day

So young

It was a horrible waste—

Stay alive because I love you

Stay alive because things will get better

Stay alive because if you don't

You won't get to see

What happens next

You'll just be forgotten

As everyone else

Moves on

And your pain

Becomes a footnote to nothing

Conventional Poem

Writing wanted me to write
        Poetry made me write this
It isn't my fault.
        Dead leaves swirling
Leaf devil haunting Fall
        Possum carcass diacritical marks
Punctuating Fall woods
        Wind-swirled leaves a comma,
Dead possum white bones an em dash —
        Maybe I'm reading too much into the woods
Maybe the woods are writing too much into me.
        Are these the woods I wandered as a child?
Where I hid when afraid
        Where I ran when joy energy
Streamed through me
        Where I cut labyrinths in the tall jewel weeds
Impossibly towering, and at the heart of the maze
        The puzzle of life
Where mystery is conceived.
        The same woods are everywhere

But now the mystery is mute

    The enigma died

Drowned in knowledge

    And yet, and yet...

That small voice

    A whisper

You know so little, it says

    We are all one

There are no barriers

    Save those in your mind.

Go to the woods

    Lie down naked on the moss

You are the trees

    You are the rocks

You are the squirrels

    The acorns

You are the worms that will eat your own flesh.

    Know this and rejoice

Know this, and that pain is an illusion

    Happiness, a mirage

Hate, a chimera

    Love, a fantasy

Know this, and that these dreams

    Comprise our deepest reality.

Get up from the moss

    Put your clothes back on

Go out of the woods

    Return to your life

Live with cautious abandon

    Poetry made me write this

It isn't your fault.

Throwing Pots

Spin, spin the wheel

Center the self

Pressing in and down.

Open up,

Begin the process,

Form your foundation.

Pull yourself up

Making the wall

That will separate you from others.

Shape that wall

It will be different

From everybody else.

Smooth your rim

Trim your base

Make your mark.

Into the fire

Then glaze

And into the fire again

Nobody knows

How it will turn out

Nobody knows

Whether it will be beautiful or ugly

Nobody knows

If it will be worth it

Your final reward

Is not in the result

But in the doing.

We Only Talked

I talked to others before

This was different

Instant connection

Electric shock

A complete understanding

And deep within me

Something started to rise

An excitement

Surroundings faded away

And in those short minutes

I knew I was falling in love.

Falling is the wrong word

For a soaring lifting flight

A jet taking off

On the runway of life

Headed for the sky.

Could I have stopped it then

Maybe it was already too late

Hearts know what they want

Even so

I was angry with myself

For being in love

With the wrong person.

But love didn't care

Lonely needs what it needs

Found a gem in an unlikely place.

Every day I looked for you

Seeing you everywhere

Marking time until you walked in

Everyone seemed to know

We were a couple

Even if we tried to hide it

Maybe we stood too close together

Maybe we just fit each other so well

We don't talk as much anymore

I suppose somewhere inside

I knew it had to end

Knew as I soared above the clouds

My landing gear was broken

The engine would stop someday

And I would fall

Not in love

Rather, into pieces

I did not care

Love took what it desired,

Gave back only memories

That jewel is on the inside now

Away from prying eyes

Looking at it sometimes

Wondering if I will ever soar again

Still dear to me always

It is no less a gem.

A part of me forever,

I cannot lose it

Even if we have lost each other.

We only talked for hours

There was so much to say

Never enough time

Never enough love.

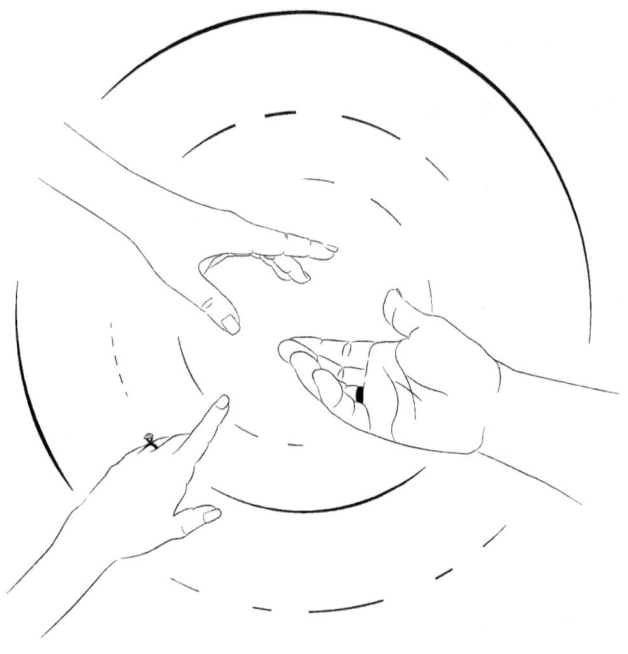

You Fall In Love

When you fall in love
You treat each other gently
Against the time
That love falters

Wind the string around the top
Throw the top at the ground
Holding one end of the string
Watch the top twirl

When you fall in love
And things aren't quite right
Not up to code
It doesn't necessarily ruin things

Not right away.

How smoothly the top turns
Balancing on point
Dancing inexorably
In graceful pirouettes

But in human relations
Something always goes wrong
Sometime.

The top rotates more slowly
Look, a slight wobble

And if one loves two
Questions of loyalty
Of priority
Of decency

Inevitably begin to intrude.

The top precesses
Erratically now
Gyrations becoming
Wild and out of control

As a cat's tail whips around to compensate
As one's arms windmill, slowly tilting over
As emotions propel the lovers in shark circles
As the top spirals down to the ground

Endings are seldom pretty.

The Alchemy of Pain

When life gives you pain

(And when does life not)

It is a gift more precious than joy

Though pleasure is nice

It leaves in a trice

While pain is a constant toy.

Learn how to use it

To change it

Amuse it

Use pain to sharpen your knife

Make friends with pain

It will show you the way

While pleasure just sits there, babbling

But how do you change it?

You ask, not believing,

Still wanting pleasure instead

Perhaps what is needed

Is a catalog of pain

Cross-referenced, indexed,

With footnotes and comments

To show you how pain can be used

Physical, emotional, spiritual pain

The pain of ignorance

The pain of knowledge

Recipe follows.

The gift of pain is a poison bread

Su dolor es mi dolor

Make croutons of the pain

Mix a salad of grief, thwarted ambition, lost love

Pour on the vinegar of regret

Add oil of failure

Sprinkle the croutons of pain on top

Eat, while reading

All the books about free will you can find

This nutritious meal

Will stay with you

Whether you like it or not.

Lost Child

Wandering in the woods

No sign of anyone

Anywhere

The woods so large

And you're so tiny.

Where are the angels

To hover over you?

Where is the firebird

To show you the path?

Fear not,

For the woods turn out to be

Smaller than you thought.

Look, a flash of light!

Listen, a flutter of wings!

The glowing feather leads you toward home

The angel enfolds you in her arms

And for a time, perhaps forever...

The wandering child is lost no more.

My Mother

Whan that Aprill, with his shoures soote
My mother would begin,
For she had memorized Chaucer,
In college for a class. She majored in French,
Was Phi Beta Kappa, and met my father-to-be there
She was his grey-eyed Athena.
I loved her as much as any child loves its mother.
She was funny and quick, liked nonsense and was sad.
But sad was later. She was a substitute teacher
Although she would have been a fine regular teacher
Her degree was not in education.
She tried to stop smoking but couldn't.
I tried to help, once.
When I was in fifth grade I had a chemistry set.
I had heard about aversion training
I figured if her cigarettes tasted bad
She would stop smoking them,
So I mixed some chemicals and
Dipped the filter ends of the cigarettes
Into the mixture, not paying attention to
The chemicals discoloring the ends of the cigarettes

Which rather worked against my plan.

I put her cigarettes back

But she noticed the discoloration

I was not punished even though

They might have thought I was trying to poison her.

Probably, they were simply baffled.

Years later, she took me to be tested

An IQ test and psychological evaluation

Because I was an underachiever.

I was furious because nobody

Had consulted me about it.

I was about twelve. They said I was smart and angry.

I could have told them that.

She had gone to Walnut Hills High School

In Cincinnati. A school that takes in

Promising students from around the area

To prepare them for college.

All students must take several years of Latin.

We lived on the west side of town,

Walnut Hills was on the east side.

I wanted to go to Walnut Hills, too.

Almost nobody from the west side goes there.

The principal at my elementary school thought

It was just because my mother had gone there.

I was called into the principal's office

So she could disabuse me

But I was ready, told her I wanted to take AP Biology

Which they didn't offer at Western Hills

Which is where I would have gone otherwise.

A friend of mine complained

Why would you want to go to Walnut Hills?

There are n____s there.

I never talked to that friend again.

I hope he's more tolerant now.

Otherwise he wouldn't like his old neighborhood

Because now there are n____s there too.

It's still a nice neighborhood.

Some of my best friends are white.

When I left home for graduate school

I told her I had been at home too long.

Not intending to hurt her

Just to convey my thoughts

But she seemed hurt anyway.

My mother had migraines,

High blood pressure, depression.

I inherited the first two, and maybe the third as well

Although I have some of

My father's insouciance to counteract it,
And my father's thin blood instead of my mother's.
I was at my in-law's house in Louisville one Christmas
When my mother had a minor heart attack.
She was in the hospital
Should we come to Cincinnati
A little bit early? I asked my father over the phone.
No, you'll be up here in a few days, he said.
Don't worry about it.

The next night she had another heart attack and died.
I stared out the windows there in Louisville
Nobody said much that I recall.

In the funeral home her closed eyes were sunken
She had donated her corneas.
My father is buried next to her now
In a family plot
That will not hold many more.

If she were here
I'd find some way to ease her depression
That got worse as she grew older.
If she were here

I'd tell her about the things I've done,

The joys, the sorrows.

If she were here

I'd help her see the beautiful, brilliant woman she was

Before time and circumstance took all that away.

If she were here

I'd tell her I love her.

If your parents are still alive

The time to do that is now.

Don't wait until they are dead

Because it's not as good.

My Father

He said, Let's say you're in a crowd, maybe in a theater.
If you stare at the back of someone's head,
They will sense it.
They'll turn around and look back at you.
Try it sometime.

So I did. He was my father, he knew things I didn't.
But was it true? If someone turns around and looks,
Does that mean they sensed me?
Or does it just mean most people look around
And if they see somebody staring at them,
They'll stare back?

He was certain that telepathy was real.
He knew that emotions could and should
Be controlled.
He usually said this when my mother
Had gotten upset about something.
How can I control what I feel? My mother asked.
Practice, seemed to be his answer,
Which was no answer really.

Some years later, Archie Bunker's rebuke
"Stifle yourself"
Appeared to capture his idea.
But my father said it more gently.
His own demeanor was almost always calm.

He got upset once when I imitated
A gay man's imagined lisp.
(In many ways I was a stupid kid.
But then that's what kids are like.)
You don't think that's funny, I said
No, I don't, he said
So I stopped. I wasn't *that* stupid. Not by then.

If you get a headache, he said,
Use willpower to conquer it.
Develop your willpower and things will get better.
When my migraines started I took his advice at first.

I know better now. So many things I know better now.

Maybe not everyone would take up science
As a way of finding out if one's father was correct.
In junior high I read Frank Edwards' books

About strange phenomena:
Fortean mysteries, spontaneous human combustion,
Ball lightning.
For many, there are now explanations.
For others, I use the wisdom embodied in the advice,
Judge whether it is more likely for the thing to be true,
Or if instead, someone is either mistaken or lying.

So many things there are to be mistaken about.

He had lost most of his hair at the front of his scalp
Except for a patch that he grew long and combed back.
Not exactly a comb-over, more like
Some odd sort of Mohawk.
My hair was different from his.
You are keeping your hair well, he said,
You must be massaging your scalp like I taught you.
No, I said. There is a thing
Called male pattern baldness.
It's genetic, I explained. He seemed surprised.

One time he said,
Remember when I told you to ignore headaches?
I was wrong. You should treat them.

By then I already knew that,
But I was impressed that he had learned.
My migraines hadn't been diagnosed yet.
They were just bad headaches.
I was thirty, he was seventy-one
And looking quite healthy.
Seventeen years later he was dead.
My father liked the book "Two Little Savages"
By Ernest Thompson Seton
About a couple of boys who decide to live in the wild.
My father became a scoutmaster
I was a Boy Scout in his troop for a while
I didn't like it and I quit.
He didn't rebuke me
But he had to stop being a scoutmaster soon after.
Maybe I disappointed him
Surely I did when I got my law degree
And rejected his offer to take me into his own practice
It was a good decision on your part, my wife said
Years before our divorce.
I never read anything by E. T. Seton
I preferred A. C. Doyle and Jules Verne
Had read The Lost World when I was in first grade
Books were my escape.

Comic books too, but my mother threw them away
Probably not really all that valuable
After I got through reading them.
However, this is about my father.
I misspelled that word as "fathat" in third grade
The mistake made me laugh convulsively for days after
Whenever I looked at that word fathat.
Fat
Hat.
My father used to wear a hat.
He worked downtown in the Pan-Am building
Until they let him go
He opened up a solo law practice then.
Never did very well.
Still, he was respected
To the extent that non-wealthy lawyers get any respect.
He taught Hatha yoga sometimes.
I could achieve the lotus position easily as a child
And so I devalued the discipline
Not anymore, on either count.
He was about to teach a yoga class when he felt dizzy,
Symptoms of a stroke.
He took some aspirin.

It was in fact a stroke, but a hemorrhagic stroke.

The aspirin didn't help.

I talked to him on the phone

When he was in the hospital.

No need to visit, he told me.

It would have been an eight-hour drive.

I stayed home.

Soon he had a second, much larger stroke.

It was in the back of his head.

Stare at it, he will turn around and look at you.

Try it sometime.

We Will Meet Again

We will meet again, you and I.
Beyond the hills, beyond the valleys,
Beyond the mountains,
Beyond the feasts and campfires and judgments.
We will meet and clasp hands and hug and laugh.
Those were the times, we will say.
We will meet again and we will talk
About all the things we have done.
We'll have a beer or two, and remember.

We'll go fossil hunting, like we wanted to,
So many years ago.
Horn coral, brachiopods, trilobites
Curled up sleepy in their limestone beds.
We'll find them and put names to them all
Knowing that the hill we stand on
Was an ancient ocean, and fall silent in wonder.

At night we'll look up at the stars,
Knowing we are here because a supernova
Billions of years ago

Gave birth to the matter that forms us
And we will feel the awe
That comes from contemplating origins.

No.
It isn't true. We will not meet again.

Never again will we hug each other.
Never again will you relate to us
The story of your experience.
Never again will you tell me that
One's feelings should be controlled,
That pain should be ignored.

Yes, you were younger when you told me that,
Younger than I am now.
We will not meet again. Not here,
Not anywhere.

Sometimes, in the quiet dark
Or noisy city street, I remember you.
They say nobody really dies
As long as they are still remembered.
People will believe what they wish.

You were good at that,
Believing what you wanted to be true
And ignoring the rest. A good skill for a lawyer,
One a scientist must avoid.
They say people can always be useful to others
Even if only to serve as a bad example.
Ah, but wait, that's too harsh.

I prefer to think I took your best advice
Merely recast it if I had to.
Think for yourself, you said.

I want to say to you,
Examine your deepest assumptions.
I want to say, perhaps feelings cannot be controlled.
I want to tell you that pain
Should not always be ignored.
We have this conversation, you and I

And I imagine that you listen.
We discuss war, religion, philosophy
And then I know, here, in my heart and mind
We will meet again.

The Uniform

He was in a coma before I got there.

Nobody knows if someone in a coma can hear you.

Some can, apparently, others cannot.

He'd had a massive cerebral hemorrhage

So I suspect the answer was no.

We told him we loved him, anyway

The doctors and nurses seemed to approve

Although the words probably only helped

Our own tortured emotions.

It will have to do.

They moved him to another hospital.

He had a living will.

It said if two doctors thought he had no chance

Of coming out of a coma

We were to pull the plug.

I was his executor-in-waiting

So it was up to me

Since my stepmother didn't want to be responsible.

(Probably a good decision on her part.)

The two doctors didn't need to think much.

Nobody, they said, had ever

Come out of a coma so deep.

There was a third who seemed to expect miracles
But we stopped my father's intravenous feeding.
After a few days his urine turned brown.
Somebody thought he should be in a hospice
At the time I didn't say how silly that idea was
This late in the game.
The woman from the hospice came to the hospital
To see if my father qualified
To see if he is actively dying she said
We had just been in his room to look at him
To watch him breathe
We waited in a different room while she went to him
She came back with a strange look.
He's dead she said
And left like an angel.
Maybe she knew how it would appear
Or maybe she just thought we were all idiots.
He had died sometime in those few minutes
After we left and before she entered.
I'm sorry/not sorry I missed it. Pick one, it will be true.
Pick both, it will be truer.

I rang Tibetan prayer bells at his funeral
And recited Invictus from memory.

He had liked that poem
For its message of being in control.
He liked to think he was in control
I guess he couldn't help it.

He had his army uniform
Left from the days of World War Two
He had a Purple Heart, a Bronze Star
He fought in Italy for a brief time
Before he was wounded by shrapnel
In his knee, his chin
Good enough for a little disability pension
Enough to buy cigarettes
Until he quit smoking.
When he was dead his uniform disappeared.
I happened to be there when my stepmother
Was setting out clothing to donate to charity.
A big rack of clothes on the porch.
As the executor, I figured my job
Was to look at all things he had owned.
I looked at the clothing that she had set out
To see if there was anything there.
What's this? A uniform, good olive drab,
Not hard to find if you look.

After that I didn't talk much with my stepmother
Our paths didn't intersect often
She'd hated guns. I respect that.

I sympathize with pacifists, not hard to do
Since war is a game for brigands and thieves
But history tells us it won't go away
Not caring how hard we wish it.
And history is precious to sons and daughters
Who grasp at whatever they can
To remember their father in their pain and grief.

For no matter how often they tell you
That life is bitter and short
That everyone dies and everyones lives
With the knowledge that ending will come
It's still a surprise when it happens to you.
It's still a surprise when your parents are dead
It's still a surprise when your time slips away
And all the poetry ends.

Notes

Forgotten Symmetry

This is the finest piece in the book, mainly because it's the only one that isn't all about Frank. Remarkably, the history appears to be accurate. He presents a couple of interesting juxtapositions involving Civil War participants and a curious coincidence concerning names. He was always fascinated by names, his own being so common and boring. This was the poem he was writing when I introduced him to my daughter Missy who was thinking of becoming a poet. However, it did not discourage her.

Child in Bathtub

Frank was a fervent supporter of anti-child-abuse causes in his later years. With this piece his intention was clearly to draw attention to cases of shaken-baby syndrome, or SBS, now sometimes termed Abusive Head Trauma. I believe he himself was somewhere on the autistic spectrum, as he often seemed unable or unwilling to look people in the eyes when he talked with them. He had a reputation of being shifty-eyed and as a result many people simply didn't trust him. He mainly complained about this when he was drunk, which was often. He said it was just too painful, too intense to look into people's eyes, and that he couldn't concentrate on the conversation if he did that. I tried to get him to learn to distance himself from people, to view them as monkeys in suits, or naked. He said that only made it worse. I should also point out that many children who have not been abused scream without apparent reason, the little brats.

Books, Books, Books

It isn't clear who the child is that he writes about here. There is no evidence that he was a child prodigy or learned to read at an unusually early age. Most likely, this piece tells the story of a childhood friend Frank met in grade school or secondary school.

Adult Education

Don't know why this is here. Maybe he took a course at a community college and this was part of the curriculum.

Becoming Rehinged

The limerick-like rhythm of these stanzas belie the apparent serious tone. During discussions at bars Frank would make Zen koan-like statements. He once said, "Science is a certain method of knowledge based on knowing nothing for certain," and similar hogwash. He thought he knew so much about things he never did. Notice he never tells us "how we know what is true." He probably never knew. Meanwhile, he told me he was trying hard to quit drinking. He said he sometimes heard voices, whispers, in faint white-noise sources like forced-air heating ducts. He associated that with psychological conflicts with his overactive superego. He sometimes spouted similar Freudian nonsense thinking it would impress people. He said in high school he was bullied, called a "fag" and "homo" because of casual associations with friends; that the nosepiece of his broken glasses was often taped with white medical tape in the classic nerd way; that later in life he was accused of making phone-sex calls from his employer's workplace. I mention these things only to suggest the depravity of the man who would elevate taking illegal drugs to the height of philosophical illumination. This surely is an instance of his conscience hitting him so hard he made up an entire fake philosophy to justify his selfish use of black-market drugs. In this perhaps he tried to emulate John C. Lilly, but Frank was merely a minor reflection of that misguided soul. He sometimes claimed that many people who took LSD in the sixties and seventies are now doctors and lawyers. But if that's true, why haven't people come forward with their stories? Besides Steve Jobs and Oliver Sacks, of course.

The Forgiving

After Frank's death I sent a copy of this poem to my daughter and she returned it, burnt to ashes. So much for the power of Frank's advice.

Love Sum

What a supremely self-indulgent load of crap. Few things are more tiresome than a list of old loves. Here, Frank probably invents at least half of these women — he's too much of a coward to actually name them, of course — assuming they are in fact all women. He enjoyed comparing conquests, even if I had to nag him repeatedly to do it. Any notion that Frank was romantic is destroyed by his comparison of love to a zombie, a creature of horror movies. All these people are no doubt thankful that he is out of their lives.

Stay Alive

Quite an ironic poem considering how he ended it all.

Conventional Poem

I don't know, some kind of neo-pseudo-Hindu-Buddhist nonsense? Seems to me he can't make up his mind whether illusions are real or not. Typically, Frank disowns any intent by saying he was made to do it. My daughter told me he wrote this when the two of them went into the woods for a picnic.

Throwing Pots

If I were the clay I would ask the potter what he was trying to make. Because, after all, the potter has a responsibility to the clay to make sure he does all he can to turn it into something wonderful, useful, and pleasing to the eye and touch. Anything less would be criminal, evil. Frank doesn't seem to get that.

We Only Talked

Found this poem in Missy's room, handwritten, signed by Frank. This was all the evidence I needed.

You Fall In Love

He talks about falling in love. I'm never sure what people are talking about when they say they fell in love. I mean, sure, you love somebody, you marry them, you have kids. What's so complicated?

The Alchemy of Pain

Now here we get an insight into what really motivates him. I always said, people who are hurt, hurt other people. You can express that more succinctly by saying, "hurt people hurt people." Get it? Now, I'm sure Frank would have said everyone gets hurt sometimes, and since everyone is a hurt person then it really doesn't mean anything. But maybe Frank was more hurt than most, okay?

Lost Child

I am certain this poem is about Frank and Missy.

My Mother

Frank's mother had been diagnosed with depression and according to him, had electric shock therapy before he was born. His grades in school were not exceptional but there is no evidence that he was an "underachiever" as claimed here; his academic career was merely undistinguished. Possibly he is trying to inflate his own importance as he has done so often in the past.

My Father

He certainly goes on and on about his father, doesn't he. I wonder how much of this is real. Frank had a vivid imagination and would make up stories about jobs he said he'd had. He once told me he'd had a job re-packaging merchandise bought by shoppers whose only job was to monitor the honesty of sales clerks; that he'd worked for the IRS, sending letters to taxpayers who had made mistakes on their tax returns. Okay, yes I knew he seduced my daughter, and I did give him that bottle of vodka, the lush, but I didn't think he would drink it all in one night. Do I care? Not really. He betrayed me, betrayed my trust, just like he betrayed anyone who ever befriended him.

We Will Meet Again

Well, will they meet again or not? Once again, Frank can't make up his mind.

The Uniform

He claimed he was drafted for the Vietnam war but was classified 4-F due to his high blood pressure which was untreated at the time. He said some people accused him of taking drugs to increase his blood pressure before the physical, but there was no reason to do that because he'd always had high blood pressure. Then he claimed his marriage failed due to sexual dysfunction caused by the blood pressure medication he was prescribed. Again, I have no idea how much of that is true. Probably he is making up a medical condition to excuse his bad behavior.

Overview

So, here at the end I'm supposed to supply some kind of summary, maybe tie everything together into a neat package. Well, Frank never was one to do that, so why should I? I'm no poet in the first place, I don't know if his stuff is any good. I'm sure Frank would have been thrilled to know his work was getting published. As though that means anything, really. It isn't like he got a huge advance and a contract to write more, for pity's sake. No, the only reason this book got published at all is because nobody had to pay the poor bastard any money. I think he really wanted to write a novel but didn't have the patience, so he wrote fiction in the form of poetry. Much shorter, no need to adjust continuity, or even provide a plot. So you see, Missy, your hero was just a loser. Please come home.

Epilogue

Frank Arcanity could have been me
He could have been you
He could have been anyone
We'll never know

But despite all his troubles
All his travails
He wrote all his poetry
For everyone here

He was kind and generous
Warm and humorous
Loving and sharing
With a sense of wonder

Everyone knows
A Frank Arcanity
That man in the back
Who never speaks up

Who always is there
For others in need
Who always is ready
To whisper a kind word
But he also is there

To fight an injustice
To call out when someone
Beats others down

Life wasn't nice
To our Frank Arcanity
They slandered him, punched him
They turned him away

Life wasn't pleasant
But he didn't surrender
He never gave up
Till his ultimate day

If there is only one thing
Frank Arcanity could tell you
It would be this:
You are more than you know.

You have the ability
To rise above the darkness
To call out to others
To show them the way

Look deep within yourself
You can climb the mountain
You can achieve greatness
You can conquer the doubt

Follow your passion
Let your heart light your path
Let your creativity shine
Let your love embrace the world

The verse of Frank Arcanity
Will support your endeavors
It will be there to help you
Chart your own voyage

Goodbye Frank Arcanity
It was good knowing you
You made my life better
For your lost child
Lives within me.

— Melissa Dechante
Composed for the funeral of Frank Arcanity

About the Author

Michael H. Dickman was born and raised in Cincinnati, Ohio. After getting a B.S. in Chemistry from the University of Cincinnati, he went to the University of California at Irvine, learned X-ray crystallography and obtained his Ph.D. in Chemistry.

Then he attended Franklin Pierce Law Center (now affiliated with the University of New Hampshire), where he received his J.D. He practiced patent law in Washington, DC for a while.

After that he went back into chemistry, doing research and teaching at Georgetown University and at Jacobs University in Bremen, Germany. He is the author or co-author of about one hundred papers published in international scientific journals, and eventually managed to teach science at the graduate, undergraduate, high school, and middle school levels in the USA. Mr. Dickman now writes puzzles, fiction, and poetry when he isn't doing ceramics or computer programming.

About the Illustrators

I have the singular pleasure of introducing the work of two very talented people who have provided the illustrations for this book. Their contrasting styles perfectly fit the contrasting themes of the text.
 - MHD

Karina Arreola is a graphic design artist living in South Pasadena, California, with her husband and three beautiful children. She loves and appreciates all of the visual arts, including user interface design for mobile apps and all of the art that goes with it. She enjoys using her abilities to create graphic illustrations for the local school district, where her kids attend.

Jarett Coyle will attend the Honors program in Mechanical Engineering at the University of Louisville in the Fall of 2016. His artworks have been exhibited at the Cox Gallery and the Kentucky Gateway Museum in Maysville, Kentucky.

You're a Fire

You're a fire in the blood
That sets my heart to singing
You're a fever in the night
That binds my soul to yours
You're the agony of distance
When we say farewell
It's nothing I can choose to ignore

You're the passion in my life
That I cannot set aside
You're the overwhelming yearning
Of the river for the sea
You touch the core of my emotions
Somewhere deep inside
It's nothing I'd ever want to ignore

You're a fire in the blood
That sets my heart to singing
You're a fever in the night
That binds my soul to yours
My words are just a poor device
To tell you how I feel
For my love is more than all this
And my life is less without you
And you're everything I want forevermore.

Acknowledgments

Michael H. Dickman wishes to thank Bill and Trina Winter for putting up with him for so long; and BB, who showed him the forest was smaller than he thought.

Karina Arreola thanks her husband and children for being her constant and greatest inspiration.

Jarett Coyle would like to thank Stephanie Martinez for being the benevolent key to so many doors in his life.

Reading Group Guide:
Questions and topics for discussion

1. Why does the collection open with *Forgotten Symmetry*? Who is lying, and why?

2. Which is worse: physical abuse or psychological abuse? Are childhood memories accurate?

3. The teacher in *Adult Education* says that races do not exist. Do you agree? If not, are you a racist? Why or why not?

4. Is the author glorifying drugs in *Becoming Rehinged*? How do you know whether something is true?

5. In *The Forgiving* the author says one must forgive one's parents. Has the author truly forgiven his parents?

6. Is the author boasting about his conquests in *Love Sum*? Why does the author wish he had told his childhood crushes he loved them? Are there people you wish you had told you love them? Why aren't you doing that right now?

7. Have you ever contemplated suicide? Is it more cowardly to go through with it, or to resolve to live? Do questions of cowardice matter when discussing suicide?

8. What is conventional about *Conventional Poem*? What is conventional or unconventional about the rest of the book?

9. What is *Throwing Pots* about?

10. Why do people fall in love? Explain.

11. In *The Alchemy of Pain* the author advises you to read "all the books about free will you can find." If you did that, would you have time to do anything else? Do you choose to have free will or is it something you are fated to have?

12. At the end, the four poems if they can be called that, are about the author's parents. Are these any more than a maudlin recounting of sorrow? If not, is that a bad thing?

13. Although the author says that the Notes were written by Samuel Dechante, they were in fact written by the fictional poet. Is the author just denigrating his own work to save critics the trouble, or is he subtly boasting he is still sexually desirable? Which one is worse?

14. The book begins with a quote by E. L. Doctorow. Does the quote apply to poetry as well as prose? Why or why not?

Afterword

As this book was going to press I found out that much of what Samuel Dechante says in his notes is simply untrue. However, due to the demands of the publisher, it was too late to do anything but add an Afterword to alert the reader to this unfortunate situation. I hesitate to condemn Mr. Dechante, because I don't know enough about what transpired between Sam and Frank to make any comment. I can't really criticize either of them. After all, if everything you knew about a person was just a selected few private moments in their life, would you know them better than if you saw them every day? If you thought you knew a person and then caught a glimpse of hitherto unknown selected moments in their life from years past, might you completely change your opinion of that person? Is it possible to be completely objective about one's own, or anyone else's life?

    Okay, that last one is easy: no, it isn't. Therefore, I feel I should apologize to anyone who knew Frank Arcanity and who knows Samuel Dechante, for the contents of this book that might shine any unwelcome light on the past that is, after all, past and mostly forgotten.

Michael H. Dickman   May, 2016

www.ingramcontent.com/pod-product-compliance
Lightning Source LLC
Chambersburg PA
CBHW070631300426
44113CB00010B/1739